THE LIVING GOSPEL

Daily Devotions for Advent 2014

R. Scott Hurd

ave maria press AMP notre dame, indiana

© 2014 by R. Scott Hurd

All rights reserved. No part of this book may be used or reproduced in any manner whatsoever, except in the case of reprints in the context of reviews, without written permission from Ave Maria Press®, Inc., P.O. Box 428, Notre Dame, IN 46556, 1-800-282-1865.

Founded in 1865, Ave Maria Press is a ministry of the United States Province of Holy Cross.

www.avemariapress.com

Paperback: ISBN-13 978-1-59471-482-5

E-book: ISBN-13 978-1-59471-483-2

Cover image "Approaching Bethlehem" © 2012 by Jeni Butler, artworkbyjeni.wix.com/art

Cover and text design by John R. Carson.

Printed and bound in the United States of America.

INTRODUCTION

Advent is a season of waiting. We wait for Christmas, when we celebrate the birth of Jesus in ancient Bethlehem and look forward to his return in glory, when he will make all things new and wipe away every tear. Advent is filled with hope as we reflect on what God has done in the past, remember what he continues to do in Christ, who is present with us now, and joyfully anticipate what our faith assures us the future will bring. This waiting time is not wasted time, but is an opportunity to live the Gospel, spread the Gospel, grow in grace, build God's kingdom, and do God's will—whatever our circumstances may be.

This book can be a useful tool as you wait and prepare for Christmas. It includes a brief devotion for each day of Advent and one for Christmas Day. Each devotion has six simple steps: (1) an invitation to be still and silent, (2) a prayer to focus you on God, (3) a selection from the gospel reading appointed for Mass that day, (4) a brief meditation to help break open God's Word, (5) a suggested action to help translate devotion into spiritual growth, and (6) a final prayer to draw you into deeper intimacy with God. These are simple devotions, intended to help you unclutter your mind and heart and pacify your days in this often too-busy season.

To benefit most from this little book, try to pray each devotion on its appointed day. You can do this at any time: with a morning cup of coffee, during a break at work, before or after daily Mass, or in bed at night before you turn out the light. Depending on your schedule and commitments, you can spend as much or as little time on each devotion as you wish. Five minutes a day is a good starting point. If time allows, it's a good idea to use a bible along with this booklet so you can read the entire reading for the day and not just the verses printed in the booklet. A notepad or journal will also be helpful to make notes or write down ideas for growth. On days when time is tight, do your best, but stretch a little—make time for what is important.

It is my prayer that this book will be a blessing to you. May it open your heart to God, help you observe a fruitful and holy Advent, inspire you to generous service, and grace your waiting with glorious hope.

Good is the Lord
to the one who waits for him,
to the soul that seeks him;
it is good to hope in silence
for the saving help of the Lord.

~Lamentations 3:25–26

Sunday, November 30
First Week of Advent

BEGIN

Be still. Be silent. Know that God is near.

PRAY

O shepherd of Israel, hearken,
from your throne upon the cherubim, shine forth.

~Psalm 80:2

LISTEN

Read Mark 13:33–37.

"Be watchful! Be alert! You do not know when the
time will come."

~Mark 13:33

Watchful and Ready

Legend has it that a traveling pilgrim once found St.
Francis of Assisi cultivating a row of beans in his garden.
The pilgrim asked Francis, "What would you be doing
right now if you knew that the world would end today?"
St. Francis smiled and replied, "I would keep on hoeing
this row of beans." Francis was so at peace with the Lord
that the prospect of meeting him didn't change his plan
for the day one bit. If someone were to ask you the same
question, how would you respond?

- Would you rush to tell certain people that you love
  them, especially those you haven't told in a while?

- Would you run to church, grab your Rosary, or make
  an act of contrition?

- Would you apologize or make amends to someone you've hurt?

- Would you make a hasty donation to charity?

- Would you start refining your excuses and polishing your alibis?

- Would you weep with regret? Would you panic or be afraid?

- Or, like St. Francis, would you be filled with peace and look forward in hope to meeting Christ?

As today's gospel reading reminds us, and as we recall urgently here at the beginning of Advent, our Lord will return on an unexpected day and at an unknown hour. He calls us to be ever-watchful and always ready, so that we aren't caught by surprise. This passage from Mark reminds us to live each day in expectation of meeting our Lord so that when he comes to us—in the ordinary times and in glory at the end of time—we can welcome him in serenity and with joy.

ACT

Take one thing off your "to do" list for today—one thing that keeps you from walking close to God. Open your eyes, heart, and mind to the presence of Christ.

PRAY

Father of Mercies, bend your ear to my pleading and teach me to stand ready to welcome Christ, whenever and wherever he comes to me. Amen.

Monday, December 1
First Week of Advent

BEGIN

Be still. Be silent. Know that God is near.

PRAY

> O shepherd of Israel, hearken,
> from your throne upon the cherubim, shine forth.
>
> ~*Psalm 80:2*

LISTEN

Read Matthew 8:5–11.

> "Lord, I am not worthy to have you enter under
> my roof; only say the word and my servant will be
> healed."
>
> ~*Matthew 8:8*

He Comes with Love

When we pray, "Lord, I am not worthy that you should enter under my roof," before receiving Holy Communion, it's not meant as a put-down. This prayer, directly inspired by the centurion's words to Jesus in today's gospel, isn't meant to imply that we are worthless, bad, or that Jesus wouldn't ordinarily have anything to do with us.

It means instead that we don't need to be found worthy in order for Jesus to enter our lives, come to be with us, or "enter under our roof." Jesus is happy to come to us; he wants to be with us, and he's delighted to receive an invitation from us. We don't have to earn his presence in our lives, because Jesus always comes in love. The love he brings is unconditional—an absolutely free and enduring gift.

At the same time, we need his love, and that's where the "not worthy" part comes in. Being "not worthy" implies we have some kind of need—a lacking. We need help. We need grace and redemption. We need hope, just like the centurion, and we need healing, just like the centurion's servant.

This is why Jesus is happy to come to us. He comes as Emmanuel, "God is with us." He comes as Jesus, "God saves." He comes as sacrament. He comes as the Eternal Word, as he did with the centurion's servant. And at Christmas, for which we wait and watch, he comes as the "word made flesh."

ACT

Consider in what area of your life you feel a lack or need for healing. Without trying to fix the problem, invite Christ to enter there.

PRAY

Shepherd of Israel, enter my wounds and heal me. Amen.

TUESDAY, DECEMBER 2
FIRST WEEK OF ADVENT

BEGIN

Be still. Be silent. Know that God is near.

PRAY

O shepherd of Israel, hearken,
from your throne upon the cherubim, shine forth.

~Psalm 80:2

LISTEN

Read Luke 10:21–24.

"Blessed are the eyes that see what you see.
For I say to you,
many prophets and kings desired to see what you
see,
but did not see it."

~Luke 10:23b–24a

Waiting in Hope

"How long until Christmas?" is often asked by children this time of year. Even though they might count down the days with an Advent calendar, their waiting can seem long and difficult. Nevertheless, their waiting is filled with hope—because Christmas always comes.

In today's gospel, we hear of people who waited. Jesus spoke of those who had longed to see what the disciples were blessed to see: the revelation of the mysteries of God's kingdom. They didn't see it in their lifetimes, but they were sustained by knowing that there would be something to be seen. For them, the future wasn't filled with uncertainty. Instead, they were filled with hope—a hope that allowed them to move into the future with confidence, and which offered a measure of joy for the present.

During Advent, we wait for the coming of Christ, the celebration of his coming among us at Christmas—when we recall his birth at Bethlehem and acknowledge his presence with us now—and his return in glory at the end of time. Our waiting isn't pointless or futile, because we believe that Jesus once came and we have faith that he will come again. This confidence for the future gives us a present hope: a hope that life has purpose and meaning because it has a destination; a hope that our brokenness now will one day be made whole; a hope that prevents us from getting stuck in past regrets; a hope that every tear will one day be wiped away; and a hope that love, which once lay in a manger, will one day reign on a throne.

ACT

Think about your biggest dream—your greatest hope. Does it fit with the peace that Christ came to establish? If not, can you let it go? How?

PRAY

Christ Jesus, teach me to live as a person of hope and to rest secure in the promise of your love, which knows no bounds. Amen.

Wednesday, December 3

First Week of Advent

BEGIN

Be still. Be silent. Know that God is near.

PRAY

O shepherd of Israel, hearken,
from your throne upon the cherubim, shine forth.

~Psalm 80:2

LISTEN

Read Matthew 15:29–37.

Great crowds came to him,
having with them the lame, the blind, the deformed,
the mute, and many others. They placed them at his
feet, and he cured them.

~Matthew 15:30

A Gift That Heals

Great crowds of people, described as "lame, blind,
deformed, and mute," came to Jesus in today's gospel
story looking for hope and healing. If you think about
it, can't we count ourselves in their number? Few of us
face their physical challenges, but we too come seeking
healing from Jesus—in the sacraments, in the Word, in
the companionship of one another—because all of us are
broken. We hurt to one degree or another.

We may come stressed by life's demands, concerned
about our relationships, under pressure to make ends
meet, or worried about our kids. We may face poor
health, loneliness, or frustrations at work. We regret poor
choices, carry baggage from our pasts, and wrestle with
compulsions and addictions. We've hurt others, others

have hurt us, and we've hurt ourselves. Whatever our circumstances, it's easy to count ourselves among the walking wounded.

We come to Jesus in our brokenness, hungry for something only he can give, and Jesus feeds us—not with loaves and fishes like the gospel crowd, but with the Eucharist, of which those loaves and fishes were a sign.

The Eucharist has been described as the "gift that heals," because in this sacrament, Jesus fills us with strength, patience, endurance, hope, forgiveness, renewed life in the Holy Spirit, and a salve for life's hurts. Above all, we receive Jesus himself, who was broken and is risen. He takes on our brokenness so that he might make us whole.

ACT

Recall an important time of healing in your life and what it taught you. How can you use that experience to lead others to Christ?

PRAY

Jesus, gentle healer, help me share your compassion this day. Amen.

WEDNESDAY, DECEMBER 3

FEAST OF ST. FRANCIS XAVIER

BEGIN

Be still. Be silent. Know that God is near.

PRAY

O shepherd of Israel, hearken,
from your throne upon the cherubim, shine forth.

~Psalm 80:2

LISTEN

Read Mark 16:15–20.

[Jesus] said to them, "Go into the whole world and
proclaim the gospel to every creature."

~Mark 16:15

Only an "Us"

Over the past several years, people of Asian, African,
Caribbean, and Hispanic descent have begun to fill the
pews of a parish I serve. Varied cultures are forming one
community, which is a beautiful thing to behold.

Sometimes, however, when different cultures meet,
there is friction, fear, racism, and resentment. Instead
of forming one community, what results is an "us and
them" type of situation. One hears comments such as,
"They're taking over our parish!" Thankfully, a better
way for Catholics of different cultures to meet is suggested by the saint we celebrate today, Francis Xavier.

Francis Xavier was one of the first Jesuits, serving as a missionary in Asia nearly five hundred years
ago. Before journeying to Japan, he met a samurai
who explained that the Japanese wouldn't embrace

Christianity overnight. Instead, they would wait to see if Francis practiced what he preached. He would need to be patient and respect the culture. St. Francis took this advice to heart. He attempted to learn Japanese, studied Japanese philosophy, and observed local customs, such as wearing a silken robe. His approach was richly blessed.

Whenever we encounter Catholics of different cultures, we do well to follow the example of St. Francis Xavier. We can seek to understand and respect their languages and cultural norms; we can learn their religious traditions and devotions; we can welcome them instead of dismissing them; we can be patient with them and with ourselves; and we can love them as the brothers and sisters that they are.

ACT

Reach out in kindness to a stranger today. Think about what his or her life situation is like. In short, notice someone new, and seek common ground.

PRAY

St. Francis Xavier, help me strive to better understand those who are not like me. May I, like you, respond to difference with warmth and welcoming. Amen.

Thursday, December 4
First Week of Advent

BEGIN

Be still. Be silent. Know that God is near.

PRAY

O shepherd of Israel, hearken,
from your throne upon the cherubim, shine forth.

~Psalm 80:2

LISTEN

Read Matthew 7:21, 24–27.

"Everyone who listens to these words of mine and
acts on them will be like a wise man who built his
house on rock."

~Matthew 7:24

Living the Word

Some two hundred years ago, a Cherokee Indian named
Drowning Bear allowed a missionary to read to him several chapters of the Bible. His reply? "It seems to be a
good book; strange that the white people are not better
after having had it for so long."

The implication here is that if people actually lived
in obedience to the Word of God, their lives would be
dramatically better as a result. This was precisely our
Lord's point in today's gospel. Jesus invites us not only
to hear his Word; he wants us also to act on it. God's
Word was not spoken simply for our information.
Instead, it's meant for our application, so that our lives
might be blessed with transformation.

Yet, in our noisy world, we can be deaf to God's
Word. In our often selfish world, it's tempting to resist

God's Word. In our skeptical world, it's fashionable to dismiss God's Word. In our overscheduled world, it's easy to neglect God's Word.

When we don't let God's Word change our lives, God lets us live with the consequences. He does so, not in vindictiveness or passive aggression, but so that we can learn to want what it is we've been missing—the freedom, peace, and wisdom that can come only from building our lives in obedience to the rock of his Word.

Let's accept the challenge of today's gospel to obey God's Word, as we prepare to celebrate at Christmas the Word made flesh.

ACT

Name one situation, relationship, or habit in your life that you think may not lead you to do what God wants of you. Create a plan—long-range or immediate—to change.

PRAY

Jesus, be on my mind, on my lips, and in my heart as I hear your holy Word. May you, who are the Word made flesh, be my constant help and protection. Amen.

FRIDAY, DECEMBER 5
FIRST WEEK OF ADVENT

BEGIN

Be still. Be silent. Know that God is near.

PRAY

O shepherd of Israel, hearken,
from your throne upon the cherubim, shine forth.

~Psalm 80:2

LISTEN

Read Matthew 9:27–31.

And their eyes were opened. Jesus warned them
sternly, "See that no one knows about this." But they
went out and spread word of him through all that
land.

~Matthew 9:30–31

Sticks in the Desert

In an ancient story, a desert monk ordered a disciple
to water a stick in the sand every day. Since the only
water source was far away, the disciple had to make a
long walk each night. After three years, however, the
stick blossomed, and the monk's community gathered
to celebrate what they called the "fruit of obedience."

Most of us would probably refuse to water a stick
in the desert because it sounds like a ridiculous thing to
do. Maybe that was the conclusion of the three men in
today's gospel. Even though Jesus had ordered them not
to tell anyone that he had healed them, they nevertheless
spread news of their cure far and wide. They probably
thought that keeping their secret was unreasonable, con-
sidering their excitement and all the questions they were

surely asked. Their actions remind us that faith involves trust that God knows what he's doing—even when his commands seem unreasonable!

Do we disregard God's commands because we think they don't make sense—things such as forgiving a hurt, loving an enemy, and living simply in a materialistic world where many starve to death each day? Do we ignore Church teachings about marriage, sexuality, and medical ethics because much of our culture says they're outdated, or even cruel? Do we fail to persevere in faith when life gets hard because we can't understand why we should? Do we do things that make us uncomfortable, but try to convince ourselves that they're okay?

Today's gospel reminds us that just because something may seem reasonable doesn't necessarily mean that it's right, and just because something is difficult to believe or seems unreasonable doesn't give us freedom to dismiss it.

ACT

Do you carry some regret? Perhaps you chose not to do something that at a deeper level you thought you should, or you did something that you really knew you shouldn't. Take that regret to prayer today. Imagine you hold it in your hands as you sit in silence before the Lord. If and when you can, release it.

PRAY

Gracious God, heal me of my lack of courage and lead me always in the path of choosing what is right. Amen.

SATURDAY, DECEMBER 6
FIRST WEEK OF ADVENT

BEGIN

Be still. Be silent. Know that God is near.

PRAY

O shepherd of Israel, hearken,
from your throne upon the cherubim, shine forth.

~Psalm 80:2

LISTEN

Read Matthew 9:35–10:1, 5a, 6–8.

[The crowds] were troubled and abandoned, like
sheep without a shepherd. Then [Jesus] said to his
disciples, "The harvest is abundant but the laborers
are few; so ask the master of the harvest to send out
laborers for his harvest."

~Matthew 9:36–38

Laborers for His Harvest

When children start to notice a number of white-bearded
men in red suits around this time of year, adults often
explain that they are "Santa's helpers." The one-and-
only real Santa is at the North Pole, of course, and he
certainly can't be everywhere at once, especially at this
very busy time of year.

Jesus couldn't be everywhere at once either. In
today's gospel, when he looked with love and compassion upon the "troubled and abandoned" crowds, he
lamented that, while the harvest was great, the laborers
were few. In other words, there was much to be done,
and Jesus needed helpers because he couldn't do it all.

He sent out his twelve apostles to help extend his ministry of preaching and healing.

The same is true in our own day. The world is filled with troubled and abandoned people, and the approaching holidays can magnify their anguish and loneliness. Jesus wants to share his love and compassion with them, and so he invites us, as he once did his disciples, to be his hands, voice, and loving mercy in our broken and aching world. Perhaps he'll work a miracle through us, but more likely our efforts will bear fruit in subtle ways, as we touch other's lives through simple gestures such as a kind word, an encouraging note, a thoughtful gift, an unexpected visit, or a shared prayer.

Today, the harvest may be as great as ever, but if we're willing to serve as Christ's helpers, we'll find that many hands make the work of his kingdom light.

ACT

Make a plan today to share Christ's presence with at least one person whom you know is troubled or feeling abandoned. Pray for this person throughout your day.

PRAY

Jesus Lord, bring me to your harvest and accept my labor for the sake of your kingdom. Teach me kindness and compassion that my life may speak to others of your abiding love. Amen.

SUNDAY, DECEMBER 7
SECOND WEEK OF ADVENT

BEGIN

Be still. Be silent. Know that God is near.

PRAY

Kindness and truth shall meet; justice and peace shall kiss.

~Psalm 85:11

LISTEN

Read Mark 1:1-8.

John the Baptist appeared in the desert proclaiming a baptism of repentance for the forgiveness of sins.

~Mark 1:4

More than Good Enough

When asked to describe himself, Pope Francis told a journalist: "A sinner." Many today would hesitate to describe themselves this way. It's easier to consider ourselves victims of society, bad parenting, unfortunate circumstances, an insensitive spouse, or lousy DNA. We may describe what we do as shortcomings, mistakes, symptoms, or even failures, but certainly not sin. Yet Jesus didn't die to save us from our shortcomings. He died to save us from our sins. That's why, in today's gospel, John the Baptist calls us to repent—to turn our lives back to God, and away from sin.

Admitting that we're sinners isn't a negative or morbid or self-hating thing to do. In fact, it can be an act of healthy self-love! When we confess that we're sinners, we accept reality, take responsibility for what we've done, and recall our fundamental need for the love and mercy of God. To call ourselves sinners doesn't mean we aren't good people. Even so, Jesus didn't call us to be good people. He called us to be holy, and that requires a serious struggle with sin.

Think of it this way: If we're concerned with simply being good, it's tempting to think that all we need to be is "good enough," which very often translates into "do no harm." That can be a very passive and self-centered approach to life. If all we need to be is "good enough," it's easy to become morally and spiritually lazy. God didn't become man in Jesus at the first Christmas so we could be "good enough." He came so that we could become one of the holy ones, and be counted among the saints.

ACT

Ask yourself, "Can I name my sins? Or does it make me uncomfortable just to think about that?" Today, look into your parish's schedule for the Sacrament of Penance and choose a time to go to confession before Christmas.

PRAY

Gentle and forgiving God, teach me to know and confront my sin that I might be ever renewed in your son, Jesus. Amen.

MONDAY, DECEMBER 8
IMMACULATE CONCEPTION

BEGIN

Be still. Be silent. Know that God is near.

PRAY

Kindness and truth shall meet; justice and peace shall kiss.

~Psalm 85:11

LISTEN

Read Luke 1:26–38.

"Behold, you will conceive in your womb and bear a son,
and you shall name him Jesus."

~Luke 1:31

What Might Yet Be

In the film *The Family Man*, Nicholas Cage's character is a wealthy businessman who had decided years earlier to leave his fiancée to pursue his professional dreams. One day he wakes up to find he's been given a glimpse of what might have been had he made a different choice. In his would-be life, he married the woman instead of leaving her. They have a happy marriage, two beautiful children, and a supportive network of friends. Having experienced this, the man comes to regret his past choices. When he's returned to his real life, he fights valiantly to restore what he has lost.

In Mary, we are given a glimpse of what might have been if the choice to sin had never been made, leaving us with a fallen human nature. Through the Immaculate Conception, God preserved Mary from this condition, allowing us to behold in her a life of perfect faith, love, and obedience to God's will. We see in Mary what we might have been.

However, Mary's witness should give us not only a longing for what might have been, but also a sign of what might yet be. Mary's Immaculate Conception made possible the virgin birth of Jesus Christ, who came to heal us and to restore what had been lost. Through Jesus, we can hope that the perfection Mary enjoyed on earth might be ours to enjoy one day in heaven. This makes today's feast not an occasion of longing and regret, but a celebration of gratitude and hope.

ACT

It's rarely too late to turn back or start over, difficult as that might be sometimes. Think of one thing in your life you wish had had a different outcome. Can you do something to redeem the situation? What can you do to draw something good out of a bad experience?

PRAY

Lord of all ages, help me see in Mary a holy model of faithful obedience to your will. Teach me to trust, submit to, and hope in you, a steady light in the darkness. Amen.

TUESDAY, DECEMBER 9
SECOND WEEK OF ADVENT

BEGIN

Be still. Be silent. Know that God is near.

PRAY

Kindness and truth shall meet; justice and peace shall kiss.

~Psalm 85:11

LISTEN

Read Matthew 18:12–14.

"What is your opinion? If a man has a hundred sheep and one of them goes astray, will he not leave the ninety-nine in the hills and go in search of the stray?"

~Matthew 18:12

No Acceptable Losses

Jesus not only tells us the beloved Parable of the Lost Sheep in today's gospel, he also asks us what we think of it. "What is your thought on this?" he says by way of introduction.

It's a good question to ponder. If we found ourselves in the shepherd's shoes, what would we do if we discovered that one sheep was missing? Would we venture out into the darkness after a hard day's work and risk twisting our ankle on a rock or falling into a thicket of thorns? If they're honest, many people might admit that they'd just as soon stay with the ninety-nine and write off the stray sheep as a loss. After all, in view of the economic ups and downs we've experienced over the past decade, the loss of one solitary sheep doesn't seem like too great a hit to a shepherd's portfolio.

Thankfully, Jesus our good shepherd doesn't view us, his sheep, through an investor's lens. Each one of us is so precious to him that there is no such thing as an "acceptable loss." When we do stray, as so many of us do, Jesus looks for us in the darkness, calling us by name, searching high and low, and doing whatever is necessary to bring us back into the safety of his fold—even if that means entering the world as a tiny baby in a stable, and dying on a cross.

ACT

Who do you see that is lost—a neighbor, friend, relative, or fellow parishioner? What can you do to help bring him or her to Christ?

PRAY

Jesus, protector of the lost, draw me ever nearer to your Sacred Heart. Teach me kindness and humility so that I may ever serve you. Amen.

WEDNESDAY, DECEMBER 10
SECOND WEEK OF ADVENT

BEGIN

Be still. Be silent. Know that God is near.

PRAY

Kindness and truth shall meet; justice and peace shall kiss.

~Psalm 85:11

LISTEN

Read Matthew 11:28–30.

"Take my yoke upon you and learn from me,
for I am meek and humble of heart;
and you will find rest for yourselves."

~Matthew 11:29

A Yoke of Rest

"Christmas would soon be at our throats," lamented P. G. Wodehouse in one of his Jeeves novels. Or, as I once read in a friend's honest, if cynical, e-mail: "Ugh. Christmas is coming. Time to get shopping."

The run-up before Christmas can indeed be a challenging time. Anxieties about finding and affording appropriate presents; the rush of decorating, wrapping, baking, and card sending; and the whirlwind of obligatory holiday parties can put people in a foul mood. The prospect of gathering with certain relatives and the journey to meet them can also add to the stress. Those without family to visit may struggle with depression. Long, dark nights and short, cold days can leave us feeling blue, a condition sometimes known as SAD: Seasonal

Affective Disorder. And many of us find ourselves worried about our pocketbooks and our jobs.

Jesus knows that we can lose our way and lose our focus when we're feeling tired, stressed, and down. That's why, in today's gospel, he invites us to learn from him, so we can find refreshment and rest, especially at this time of year. His teaching, or what he calls his "yoke," helps us put into perspective everything we're facing. The consolation of this truth gives us courage and hope, and it reminds us of who we are and what Christmas, and all of life, is about.

In other words, Christmas doesn't need to be at our throats as long as we place Christ's yoke upon our shoulders and learn from him how to find rest.

ACT

Make time today to sit still and in silence for fifteen minutes. You may find this surprisingly hard to do, but try it. Let the silence fill you and reorient your priorities.

PRAY

O my Jesus, envelop me in your tender care and help me find sweet rest. Amen.

THURSDAY, DECEMBER 11
SECOND WEEK OF ADVENT

BEGIN

Be still. Be silent. Know that God is near.

PRAY

Kindness and truth shall meet; justice and peace shall kiss.

~Psalm 85:11

LISTEN

Read Matthew 11:11–15.

"Among those born of women there has been none greater than John the Baptist; yet the least in the kingdom of heaven is greater than he."

~Matthew 11:11

Beating the Blues

Have you or someone you love ever felt depressed before Christmas? If so, today's message of hope is for you.

The gospel passage was initially written for followers of John the Baptist, so that they might become Christians. In essence, the message for them was this: (1) we know that you're sincere people of faith; (2) you should be looking for Jesus; (3) there are people and things that will try to get in the way of that; (4) don't be discouraged.

However, this is also a good message for us during this holiday season. We're sincere people of faith, and we know we should be trying to grow closer to Jesus during Advent. Yet, we have to contend with lots of people and things that can get in the way of that, and which often contribute to those holiday blues.

So what is there to do? Five things can help:

1. Lower your expectations. Remember that Jesus only got three gifts, the wise men showed up late, his family wound up in a stable, and then Herod tried to kill him.

2. Simplify, simplify, simplify! We can't do it all, nor should we try.

3. Take the high road when dealing with difficult people, because the low road never lifts anybody up.

4. Reach out to someone if you're feeling lonely, because you're not the only one who is.

5. Most importantly, never forget that Jesus and the light he brings truly is the reason for the season.

ACT

Decide on three concrete, specific things you can do in response to the list above. Make plans to accomplish these before the end of this week.

PRAY

God of compassion, fill my heart with your peace. Free me from anxiety and let me not know despair. Comfort me and heal me. Amen.

FRIDAY, DECEMBER 12
SECOND WEEK OF ADVENT

BEGIN

Be still. Be silent. Know that God is near.

PRAY

Kindness and truth shall meet; justice and peace shall kiss.

~Psalm 85:11

LISTEN

Read Matthew 11:16–19.

"To what shall I compare this generation?
It is like children who sit in marketplaces and call to one another,
'We played the flute for you, but you did not dance,
we sang a dirge but you did not mourn.'"

~Matthew 11:16–17

Straining to Hear

This time of year is an especially noisy one. Some of this noise we might call positive noise: Christmas carols, holiday music, the sounds of our favorite movies and shows, the excitement and laughter of children. Other noise, however, we might characterize as negative, namely the full-scale marketing assault we're bombarded with all day, everyday.

The danger with all this noise—both positive and negative—is that it can drown out the voice of God. His is a voice that rarely shouts; it usually speaks in whispers because, to hear a whisper, we need to give the speaker our full and undivided attention. God doesn't want his voice to get lost in all the Christmas confusion! That's why we need to make a special effort to listen amid the hubbub of this season.

Consider today's gospel. Jesus laments that the people of his generation didn't make an effort to listen to John the Baptist, or to Jesus himself. As a consequence, they robbed themselves of great wisdom.

Jesus dearly wanted them to listen, and he dearly wants us to listen as he speaks to us in the quiet corners of our hearts. Yet, in this season, silence isn't going to find us; we have to go and find it. Just think about it: when were the abiding shepherds able to hear the herald angels sing? In the middle of a silent night.

ACT

Make room in your life for quiet time with God. Think about your daily routine. Where can you begin to build in prayer time each day? If you already have that, in what other ways can you create space for silence in solitude before Christmas?

PRAY

God of song and silence, my heart rejoices in your presence. Fill me with unceasing gratitude so that I may hear and follow your gentle call. Amen.

FRIDAY, DECEMBER 12

FEAST OF OUR LADY OF GUADALUPE

BEGIN

Be still. Be silent. Know that God is near.

PRAY

Kindness and truth shall meet; justice and peace shall kiss.

~Psalm 85:11

LISTEN

Read Luke 1:39–47.

Elizabeth, filled with the Holy Spirit, cried out in a loud voice and said,
"Most blessed are you among women, and blessed is the fruit of your womb."

~Luke 1:41b–42

Our Help and Protection

On a small hill outside Mexico City, nearly half a millennium ago, Our Lady of Guadalupe's appearances to Juan Diego were a sign of the birth of Christianity in the Americas. It's for this reason that she appeared as an expectant mother, wearing a traditional, native maternity belt. Her appearance as a young Aztec woman, a member of a conquered and oppressed people, was a sign that through the Christian faith there was hope for unity and peace between the recently-arrived Spaniards, the native peoples of Mexico, and those of mixed ancestry—three groups separated by animosity, prejudice, and the wounds of history.

This hope for unity and peace is needed as much today as it was back then. Hostilities, divisions, and prejudices between peoples are found on every continent, sometimes simmering under the surface, at other times erupting in open conflict. This is as true of the Americas, whose patroness is Our Lady of Guadalupe, as it is anywhere else. Thus, the message and the mission of Our Lady of Guadalupe are both universal and contemporary.

The hope Our Lady of Guadalupe brought is grounded in love. As she explained to Juan Diego, she came to "show and make known and give all my love, my compassion, my help, and my protection to the people." In our broken world this day, we cry out to Our Lady of Guadalupe, so that the love she came to bring may heal and unite what hatred and ignorance have driven apart.

ACT

Where is there conflict and division in your neighborhood, city, or town? Who is forced to live on the margins? Today, decide on one step you will take to be a healing agent in just one of these situations.

PRAY

Our Lady of Guadalupe, teach me to bring hope and courage to those in need. May I mirror Christ in my words and actions today and all days. Amen.

Saturday, December 13
Second Week of Advent

BEGIN

Be still. Be silent. Know that God is near.

PRAY

Kindness and truth shall meet; justice and peace shall kiss.

~Psalm 85:11

LISTEN

Read Matthew 17:9a, 10–13.

"I tell you that Elijah has already come,
and they did not recognize him but did to him whatever they pleased.
So also will the Son of Man suffer at their hands."

~Matthew 17:12

From Crib to Cross

Very often, when we teach children about the meaning of Christmas, we stress the fact that it's our yearly cele-bration of Jesus' birth. In Catholic schools and religious-education programs, children sometimes sing "Happy Birthday" to Jesus and share a birthday cake, which is certainly appropriate and fun! After all, the Church's proper name for the feast is the "Nativity of the Lord." The term nativity means "birth," especially the place, process, or circumstances of a birth.

However, the primary object of Christmas is not simply to recall Jesus' birth long ago in Bethlehem but to celebrate God's saving deeds in human history, as today's gospel reminds us. We heard Jesus speak of the martyrdom of John the Baptist and predict his own passion as well. At first thought, such a reading might seem more appropriate for Lent than for Advent. Yet, it's important to recall that God came to us in Jesus to share our human condition and to save us from our sins. Jesus came for the Cross. To overlook this is to lose sight of the full significance of Christmas. Christmas is indeed a commemoration of the holy birth, but most of all, it's a feast of our redemption.

Should this recognition put a damper on our upcoming Christmas celebrations? Not at all—in fact, it ultimately serves to strengthen our hope, which is always a cause for rejoicing. Bethlehem may indeed have led to Calvary, but Calvary led to an empty tomb.

ACT

From what sin do you want to be delivered today? How can you make that happen? Is getting to confession possible? Is asking for forgiveness in order? Is reaching out to begin mending a harmed relationship needed?

PRAY

Lord Jesus, you came to redeem us, to free us from all sin. Guide me this day to turn away from sin and to set my eyes and heart on your sweet mercy. Amen.

SATURDAY, DECEMBER 13
FEAST OF ST. LUCY

BEGIN

Be still. Be silent. Know that God is near.

PRAY

Kindness and truth shall meet; justice and peace shall kiss.

~Psalm 85:11

LISTEN

Read Matthew 25:1–13.

"The kingdom of heaven will be like ten virgins who took their lamps and went out to meet the bridegroom."

~Matthew 25:1

Light for the World

A few years back, the plain white lights on my family's Christmas tree were replaced by good, old-fashioned colored lights—that can blink! And we love it.

We see lights everywhere this time of year. That's why it's sometimes called a "season of light." That was true even long before the introduction of electricity, thanks in part to St. Lucy, the fourth-century martyr whose memorial we celebrate today.

Tradition tells us that Lucy wished from an early age to consecrate her life to God as a virgin. A spurned pagan suitor, however, turned her over to the Roman authorities for being a Christian. Lucy was then forced into prostitution, but refusing to comply, she was tortured and had her eyes gouged out.

Lucy's witness to Christ led to her being blinded and deprived of receiving the gift of light. Appropriately, for centuries her feast has been celebrated at the darkest time of the year. In her honor, traditions arose which celebrate light: Lucy fires would burn in ovens, Lucy candles were lit in homes; and in Scandinavia even today, girls process with candles or a wreath of candles on their heads. Indeed, her very name, *Lucia*, in Latin means "light."

Light is always welcome during these dark days, and all the lights we may see—white or colored, blinking or not, flame or electric—are meant to be enjoyed. But like St. Lucy herself, all of them ought to point us to the one whose birth we anticipate: Jesus Christ, Light of the World.

ACT

Carve out at least fifteen minutes today to sit still and enjoy holiday lights. Perhaps you can sit with family members around the light of your Advent wreath or Christmas tree, or you can enjoy a candlelit meal. Also, choose one way to be a light for someone today.

PRAY

God of light, shatter the darkness of my complacency and teach me to be your presence to each person I encounter this day. Amen.

SUNDAY, DECEMBER 14
THIRD WEEK OF ADVENT

BEGIN

Be still. Be silent. Know that God is near.

PRAY

The Spirit of the Lord is upon me,
because he has anointed me to bring glad tidings to
the poor.

~Isaiah 61:1

LISTEN

Read John 1:6–8, 19–28.

"A man named John was sent from God.
He was not the light, but came to testify to the light."

~John 1:6, 8

Servant, Not Celebrity

When asked by a television reporter what they would
choose if they could wave a magic wand and make themselves smarter, stronger, more beautiful, or more famous,
the vast majority of those questioned chose fame.

As this little survey indicates, our culture glori-
fies fame and celebrity, tempting us to draw attention
to ourselves. What a contrast to John the Baptist! He
spent years living in a desert, where there was no one
to impress. When he returned, as today's gospel makes
clear, he did so not to point to himself but to Jesus.

John serves as a role model for us because, regardless
of our circumstances or place in society, we are meant to
glorify Jesus instead of ourselves. As Christians, we're
called to be servants, not celebrities. To do this, we need

to think of others more than we think about ourselves. We can't be servants if we're full of ourselves.

We'll know we're on the right track when we stop worrying about how we appear to other people and what they think of us. Instead, by following the lead of John the Baptist, we'll care only for what God thinks of us and be concerned only about how we appear before the Lord. At the end of the day, that's all that really matters.

> For what a man is before God, that he is
> and nothing more.
>
> ~*St. Francis of Assisi*

ACT

Write down the five things you are most proud of in your life. Do these things draw you and others closer to God? If not, what small steps can you take to shift your priorities?

PRAY

Lord Jesus, teach me to give priority to the work of your kingdom—works of justice and peace. May my faithful discipleship be my greatest source of pride. Amen.

MONDAY, DECEMBER 15
THIRD WEEK OF ADVENT

BEGIN

Be still. Be silent. Know that God is near.

PRAY

The Spirit of the Lord is upon me,
because he has anointed me to bring glad tidings to
the poor.

~Isaiah 61:1

LISTEN

Read Matthew 21:23–27.

"If we say 'Of heavenly origin,' he will say to us,
'Then why did you not believe him?'
But if we say, 'Of human origin,' we fear the crowd,
for they all regard John as a prophet."

~Matthew 21:25b–26

Whole and Complete

When a couple is too afraid, too angry, or too embarrassed to communicate honestly about difficulties in their relationship, they'll inevitably drift apart. The same is true of our relationship with Jesus. If we find ourselves too afraid, angry, or embarrassed to share parts of our lives with Jesus, our relationship with him will remain distant and superficial at best, or at worst it will completely fall apart.

This is implied in today's gospel. Jesus was told, in essence, "Tell us who you are." Jesus replied that he would gladly do so, provided that those who asked would honestly answer one simple question about John the Baptist.

Some were too afraid of what the crowd might think. Others were too embarrassed to admit they thought that John's ministry was inspired by God. Seemingly all of them were angry with Jesus because they saw him as threatening their authority. So they lied instead of honestly sharing their opinions, and their relationship with Jesus became even worse than it already was.

Today's gospel reading challenges us to review our lives and see if there are things we don't share with Jesus. If there are, our relationships with him are going to get stuck or deteriorate. Jesus has already given all of himself to us, on the Cross and in the Eucharist. In return, he asks that we give our whole, complete, authentic selves to him. After all, we're only as sick as our secrets, and we're only as intimate as we are honest.

ACT

Confront one of your secrets today. Share it with a trusted friend if you can, and speak of it to Jesus in prayer. Sit with it and think about how it holds you captive. How can you let it go?

PRAY

Gentle Savior, protect me from my darkest anxiety. Let me cling to you in hope that you will free me from all harm, if only I let you in. Amen.

TUESDAY, DECEMBER 16
THIRD WEEK OF ADVENT

BEGIN

Be still. Be silent. Know that God is near.

PRAY

The Spirit of the Lord is upon me,
because he has anointed me to bring glad tidings to
the poor.

~Isaiah 61:1

LISTEN

Read Matthew 21:28–32.

"When John came to you in the way of righteousness,
you did not believe him; but tax collectors and prostitutes did.
Yet even when you saw that,
you did not later change your minds and believe
him."

~Matthew 21:32

Living to Change

Conventional wisdom insists that "change is good."
Nevertheless, we often resist change. It seems so much
easier to stay just the way we are. Real, positive, and
meaningful change often requires both effort and sacrifice. It forces us to move out of our comfort zones, and
it requires the humility to admit that we're anything
but perfect.

However, Jesus insists in today's gospel that change
is essential—for everyone. He was speaking to a group
of elders and priests, committed religious people, just
like us. Jesus criticized them because when they heard

the truth proclaimed by John the Baptist, they didn't "change their minds."

Maybe they thought that since they were making a reasonable effort to practice their religion, unlike so many other people, they didn't really need to change. You and I can sometimes think this way, too.

That's why Jesus challenges us to continually change our minds—literally, to repent—every day. Through the Holy Spirit's inspiration, he invites us to change the way we think about ourselves, the purpose of our lives, other people, sin, and even God himself. We need to draw close in prayer to the mind of God, to conform our will more perfectly to God's will, and to let our emotions, convictions, and actions reflect what we know of God.

"To live is to change," wrote Blessed John Henry Newman, "and to be perfect is to have changed often." Continual transformation is our goal.

ACT

Identify one habit or attitude that keeps you from being the person God calls you to be. Make a plan today—and write it down—to change.

PRAY

Loving God, give me courage to change—to align my thoughts, words, and actions more closely to your will. Amen.

WEDNESDAY, DECEMBER 17
THIRD WEEK OF ADVENT

BEGIN

Be still. Be silent. Know that God is near.

PRAY

The Spirit of the Lord is upon me,
because he has anointed me to bring glad tidings to
the poor.

~Isaiah 61:1

LISTEN

Read Matthew 1:1–17.

The book of the genealogy of Jesus Christ,
the Son of David, the Son of Abraham.

~Matthew 1:1

A Complicated Cast

A television preacher once confessed to his congregation
that he hadn't read the entire Bible because he always
skipped the genealogies to get to what he thought was
more interesting stuff.

It's tempting for us to do this when it comes to Jesus'
family tree. However, a close look reveals that it includes
a fascinating and complex cast of characters: men and
women, Jews and Gentiles, the famous and the obscure.
The list includes prophets and poets, sages and shepherds, musicians and soldiers, kings and prostitutes,
teachers and builders, carpenters and farmers, civil servants and priests. Not all of them were saints; the Good
Shepherd's ancestors include a fair share of black sheep.
Their legacies include murder, adultery, cowardice,
idolatry, lust, corruption, arrogance, and faithlessness.

Nevertheless, God used every one of these diverse and imperfect individuals to accomplish his plan and prepare for the coming of his Son into the world.

You and I are also part of Jesus' family tree, and we are just as diverse and imperfect a group as his ancestors. But, just as he did with them, God seeks us, regardless of our gender, race, position, occupation, or gifts—even our weakness and sin—to help make his Son present again to a waiting and broken world.

At times, we might fear that God could not, would not, or should not call us for his purposes. But Jesus' family tells us otherwise. God wants each of us to join in the work of his kingdom. That's why he made us in the first place.

ACT

What gifts, talents, or other resources do you have to use in serving God? What can you do this week to further the work of his kingdom?

PRAY

Father of all, fill me with your wisdom so that I might understand your will for me. Give me courage to assume the place you have prepared for me among the holy ones. Amen.

Thursday, December 18
Third Week of Advent

BEGIN

Be still. Be silent. Know that God is near.

PRAY

The Spirit of the Lord is upon me,
because he has anointed me to bring glad tidings to
the poor.

~Isaiah 61:1

LISTEN

Read Matthew 1:18–25.

Behold, the virgin shall be with child and bear a son,
and they shall name him Emmanuel, which means
"God is with us."

~Matthew 1:23

Our Reason for Rejoicing

Our television airwaves are filled with images of happy
people rejoicing over the Christmas gifts they receive.
We see excited children under the tree, frantically tearing
off wrapping paper to reveal a longed-for treasure; wives
wide-eyed with amazement at a shiny new car gleaming
in the driveway; and suburban dads smiling behind the
wheel of a new riding lawnmower.

Our gospel reading for today reminds us that we as
Christians have something far more precious to rejoice
in this time of year—the gift of Christ. His holy birth in
ancient Bethlehem speaks to us of God's unshakable,
faithful, tender, merciful, and eternal love for us like
nothing else can. This is a love that will never forsake us,
never reject us; a love that always keeps its promises; a

love that never ends; and a love that comes to us without conditions or exceptions, no strings attached. God's is a love that we can name—Emmanuel, "God is with us"—because it came to dwell with us here as a person. It is a love that saves us from our sins so that we might dwell together with him forever.

This season, some may try to convince us that "nothing says 'I love you' like a diamond." But we know that nothing says "I love you" more than a newborn king. In gratitude, let's ensure that our greatest rejoicing this Christmas be not for a gift that came in a box but for the one that lay in a manger.

ACT

Think about your plans for Christmas Day. Do they allow for the focus to be on the things that really matter most in the life of a follower of Christ? If not, how can you simplify things?

PRAY

Gracious God, keep me mindful of your love this season. May all I do reflect Emmanuel—"God is with us." Amen.

FRIDAY, DECEMBER 19
THIRD WEEK OF ADVENT

BEGIN

Be still. Be silent. Know that God is near.

PRAY

The Spirit of the Lord is upon me,
because he has anointed me to bring glad tidings to
the poor.

~Isaiah 61:1

LISTEN

Read Luke 1:5–25.

"Your wife Elizabeth will bear you a son, and you
shall name him John.
And you will have joy and gladness, and many will
rejoice at his birth,
for he will be great in the sight of the Lord."

~Luke 1:13b–15a

Living for Jesus

Today's gospel recalls the announcement by the angel
Gabriel of the birth of John the Baptist. We don't decorate
trees, send cards, sing carols, or exchange presents to
mark this day as we'll do to celebrate Jesus' birth in just
six days' time. I don't think that John would mind this
a bit, because he was a humble man and clearly recog-
nized his relationship to Jesus. You'll recall that he once
said, "He must increase, but I must decrease."

John the Baptist knew that his mission was to prepare the way for Jesus. He lived his life, not to promote himself, but to promote the Lord. In this, John
the Baptist is an important witness for us, and his

example challenges our society's preoccupation with self-promotion. He reminds us that Christians shouldn't aspire to be celebrities but should strive to be servants. We should live lives that shout not "Look at me!" but "Look to Jesus!"

This is not to say that John the Baptist was not important. He was incredibly important! That's why each of the four gospels begins the story of Jesus' public ministry by first telling the story of John. You and I may be called to positions of importance: in the workplace, in society, or in the Church. But there's a big difference between being important and being self-important. St. John the Baptist bears witness to that. May we like him live our lives for Jesus, not for ourselves.

ACT

Choose one thing you will do today to point someone to the love of Christ. At day's end, examine how well you did this. If not so well, try again tomorrow.

PRAY

St. John the Baptist, teach me to have courage in proclaiming through the way I treat others that Christ comes to save. Amen.

Saturday, December 20
Third Week of Advent

BEGIN

Be still. Be silent. Know that God is near.

PRAY

The Spirit of the Lord is upon me,
because he has anointed me to bring glad tidings to
the poor.

~Isaiah 61:1

LISTEN

Read Luke 1:26–38.

Then the angel said to her,
"Do not be afraid, Mary, for you have found favor
with God."

~Luke 1:30

Be Not Afraid

First-time moms and dads are often excited and appre-
hensive at the same time. They may worry: "Am I up
to the job? How will I juggle work and family? Will my
baby be okay? How is my life going to change? Can we
afford this?"

Consider how Mary may have felt at the Annun-
ciation. It was an angel who told her that she'd be a
mom. What's more, he said she wouldn't be an ordinary
mom—her son was to be a king! To top it off, she wasn't
even married yet, and somehow her child was to be con-
ceived by a "Holy Spirit."

Scripture describes Mary as frightened and con-
fused, and who could blame her? Thankfully, Gabriel

understood. He told Mary to put away her fears, and he assured her that nothing is impossible for God.

Aren't Gabriel's words meant for us, too? Like Mary, we may face situations that fill us with fear, appear impossible, or seem to make no sense, and we wonder how they fit into God's plan. We may find ourselves asking Mary's question: "How can this be?"

When we do, Mary invites us to imitate her surrender, entrusting ourselves into the hands of a trustworthy God by saying, "Your will be done." Even though we may be afraid, even though we may not understand, even though the way ahead looks dark, still we should trust, as she did.

To know "the Lord is with you" was enough for Mary, and it can be enough for us, too.

ACT

How can you share the call to trust that is inherent in the Christian life? Think about someone you know who is struggling, and discover a way to help him or her find the courage to trust that all will be well because God is good.

PRAY

God of compassion, help me first confront the dark corners of my own life, with confidence that you will be with me. Then teach me to be a loving witness to others who are fearful. Amen.

SUNDAY, DECEMBER 21
FOURTH WEEK OF ADVENT

BEGIN

Be still. Be silent. Know that God is near.

PRAY

Behold, I am the handmaid of the Lord.
May it be done to me according to your word.

~Luke 1:38

LISTEN

Read Luke 1:26–38.

Mary said, "Behold, I am the handmaid of the Lord.
May it be done to me according to your word."

~Luke 1:38

More than Belief

Many jokes are told about men's fear of commitment, but the truth is that both men and women can hesitate to commit because they've been hurt or disappointed somewhere along the way. They find it hard to trust, since they've learned that not everyone is trustworthy. Promises have been broken; lies have been told; parents, lovers, and friends have let them down. As a result, they may fear committing themselves to God.

If that's true of us, Mary's witness can offer encouragement. When Gabriel announced that she had been chosen to be the Mother of God, she didn't know what she was signing on for. Gabriel didn't give her a picture of what the future would hold. He simply met her in the present and asked, "Will you do this?" And Mary answered, "Yes." She agreed without exceptions or limits, with no "ifs, ands, or buts." She didn't request a trial period or say, "Let's wait and see." Instead, she committed without conditions and moved forward in faith. Mary wasn't being impulsive or foolhardy. She knew that Gabriel spoke for God and that God is trustworthy.

Mary's unwavering commitment reminds us that faith is more than just belief. Most of all, faith is about trust—trust that God never breaks his promises, that his love for us is undying, and that he himself is faithful without fail. The world around us may indeed let us down, but, as Mary knew, God never will.

ACT

Recall a time in your life when you were able to see God's faithfulness at work. Each time you recall the story today, pause and offer thanks. Then find a way to share the trust you learned from that experience.

PRAY

Faithful Lord, continue to shower me with your grace. Help me place my trust in you every day, every hour. Amen.

Monday, December 22
Fourth Week of Advent

BEGIN

Be still. Be silent. Know that God is near.

PRAY

Behold, I am the handmaid of the Lord.
May it be done to me according to your word.

~Luke 1:38

LISTEN

Read Luke 1:46–56.

"He has thrown down the rulers from their thrones
but lifted up the lowly.
The hungry he has filled with good things;
the rich he has sent away empty."

~Luke 1:52–53

Magnify the Lord

Beautiful music is a rich blessing of this time of year.
More than any other season, Christmastime is marked
by its music—familiar songs, both secular and religious.
We all have our favorites, and many of us can't help but
sing them as we go about these days.

Today's gospel presents to us what we might consider to be the first Christmas song, Mary's *Magnificat*.
The hymn's name comes from its first line, in Latin,
which is often rendered, "My soul magnifies the Lord."
What is interesting for a Christmas song, however, is
that Christ isn't mentioned. Mary sings about herself
a little bit, but more importantly, she sings about what
God the Father has done for her. Most of all, her song is
about what God the Father has done for all of humanity.

Mary's Magnificat is a celebration of God's breaking into the world, in order to stand the world on its head. God's Son comes in Jesus to remake the world in the way he intended it to be in the first place, before we messed things up. The mighty are cast down; the humble are exalted. The hungry are fed; the rich are sent away hungry. For all of this, Luke has Mary announcing that her soul seeks to magnify the Lord and all his mighty works. Mary is striving to spread the incredible news of God's goodness, his justice, and his peace, and we are to do the very same thing.

This is a hopeful message, and it's a challenging one. It is hopeful because it celebrates God's coming to set things straight, but it's challenging to those who might need to be set straight or to help with the straightening. We who are citizens of one of the world's richest nations may find this especially challenging, since standing the world on its head may mean great sacrifice for us.

Mary's Magnificat recalls that while God came to comfort the afflicted, God also came to afflict the comfortable. Our job, like hers, is to magnify this incredible news by how we live and pray and maybe even by how we sing.

ACT

Listen closely to one of your favorite religious Christmas songs. What does it mean for you? What do the words say to you about how we are to live as Catholic Christians? Reflect throughout the day on the ways music shapes us and teaches us to be faithful people.

PRAY

God of justice, stir in me a desire to magnify your greatness in everything I do today. Let song fill my heart and praise of you be ever on my lips. Amen.

Tuesday, December 23
Fourth Week of Advent

BEGIN

Be still. Be silent. Know that God is near.

PRAY

Behold, I am the handmaid of the Lord.
May it be done to me according to your word.

~Luke 1:38

LISTEN

Read Luke 1:57–66.

All who heard these things took them to heart,
saying,
"What, then, will this child be?"
For surely the hand of the Lord was with him.

~Luke 1:66

A Proper Perspective

For many, Christmas is a warm, happy, nostalgic, and
sentimental time —and that's good. It is our celebration
of the birth of our Savior, after all, and it is right for us
to enjoy it. At the same time, we don't wish to trivialize
Christmas and overlook the truly awe-inspiring significance of what we commemorate.

Today's gospel can help us regain a proper perspective on Christmas. Zechariah and Elizabeth's neighbors
knew that something wonderful was happening as the
events of John the Baptist's birth unfolded before them.
We're told that at first they rejoiced; then they were
amazed; and finally, they were filled with fear, since
they could see that the hand of the Lord was at work in
powerful and unexpected ways.

The emotional reactions of these gospel characters to the birth of the Baptist can challenge us to reconsider our response to Jesus' birth. They remind us that, in him, the creator of the universe shivered in straw;

> the all-knowing one had to learn to crawl and walk;
> the all-powerful one became helpless;
> the all-holy one dwelt among the unholy;
> he who needs nothing became dependent on a mother and a father;
> the King of Kings and Lord of Lords entered our world in obscurity and poverty;
> divinity joined with humanity;
> and our hope for redemption rested in the tiniest of hands.

Should we reflect on such things, we may find ourselves, like Elizabeth and Zechariah's neighbors, filled with joy, amazement, and holy fear at the unexpected and awe-inspiring acts of God. Like them, we do well to take these things to heart and continue to wonder.

ACT

Carve out fifteen minutes today to contemplate the birth of Christ. Really think about this: God became human. God became the most fragile, vulnerable, and weakest of humans. Ask yourself: Why? What does it mean? Don't settle for a response that someone else has articulated. What does it mean for you?

PRAY

God of love, fill my heart with sweet wonder this day. Amen.

WEDNESDAY, DECEMBER 24
CHRISTMAS EVE

BEGIN

Be still. Be silent. Know that God is near.

PRAY

O Radiant Dawn,
splendor of eternal light, sun of justice:
come and shine on those who dwell in darkness.

LISTEN

Read Luke 1:67–79.

"And you, child, will be called the prophet of the
Most High,
for you will go before the Lord to prepare his way."

~*Luke 1:76*

The Lights Are Up

Concertgoers know that the show is about to begin as
soon as the house lights go dark and the stage lights go
up. Excitement mounts—usually someone in the audi-
ence claps or yells—because what they've been waiting
for is about to start.

Zechariah expresses a similar excitement in today's
gospel, in his hymn that tradition calls the *Benedictus.* He
and the people of Israel had been waiting—for God to
fulfill his promises, free them with his mercy and salvation, and guide them in the ways of holiness, righteousness, and peace. In his son, John the Baptist, it was as if
the lights went up on stage because he was to prepare
the way for Jesus, the "daybreak from on high," who
would shine on those who sit in darkness. Zechariah
was overjoyed that the wait was over, and he praised

God for it. Perhaps we can even imagine him clapping while he sang.

Our Advent waiting has taken place during the darkest time of the year. But now, as Christmas is about to arrive, the days begin to get longer and light begins to replace the darkness. We're filled with excitement, since the Christmas we've been anticipating is almost here. Like Zechariah, we rejoice and praise our gracious God.

It's said that good things come to those who wait, and there's nothing better to wait for than the coming of Christ—his coming not just in memory but in our everyday lives and in our promised future. The lights have gone up; the wait is almost over! Our Advent hope will soon be filled with Christmas joy.

ACT

What is your greatest joy this Christmas? Commit to one act by which you will share its blessing with another person or group of people. Make a concrete plan to do this before the Church's celebration of the Christmas season ends on January 11.

PRAY

God of rejoicing, shatter the darkness of my world with the radiant light of your Son. Teach me to be a bearer of his light. Amen.

THURSDAY, DECEMBER 25
THE NATIVITY OF THE LORD (CHRISTMAS)

BEGIN

Be still. Be silent. Know that God is near.

PRAY

I proclaim to you good news of great joy:
Today a Savior is born for us,
Christ the Lord.

~Luke 2:10–11

LISTEN

Read Luke 2:1–14.

While they were there, the time came for her to have
her child,
and she gave birth to her firstborn son.
She wrapped him in swaddling clothes and laid him
in a manger.

~Luke 2:6–7a

Hope in the Bleakest Night

Many artistic depictions of Christmas present a sanitized
and romantic scene in the Bethlehem stable. Mary and
Joseph, looking remarkably rested and refreshed, clean
and well dressed, kneel beside the swaddled infant Jesus,
cradled in sweet-smelling straw, while adoring shepherds and gentle beasts look on in wide-eyed wonder.

In reality, however, Mary and Joseph would have
been worn out from their ordeal. The manger straw was
likely crawling with pests, and the animals would have
been filthy and indifferent. As for the shepherds—they
had a reputation for being rough, even criminal. It's been
suggested that the birth in that stable and a visit by those

shepherds would be like delivering a child in a bus station in the middle of the night and having a street gang come to visit.

The birth of Jesus in Bethlehem might seem a rather bleak and hopeless occurrence. Yet, we Christians find in it great hope and cause for joy. The newborn infant, lying in the cold night, is none other than the Son of God, who came to bring salvation for all people. It is this that caused the shepherds to shout for joy and offer glory and praise to God. It is upon this that Mary prayerfully and silently reflected in her heart. And it is this that can bless us with hope, even in seemingly hopeless situations. In the midst of even our darkest nights, Christ is there.

ACT

Who in your city or town is suffering a bleak and desperate time this Christmas season? How can you help to create, not just a quick fix, but a long-term solution to the root of the problem? Today may seem to be the wrong time to discuss or plan for this kind of action, but truly it is the perfect day.

PRAY

Holy Child of Bethlehem, fill my heart with compassion and clarity of purpose on this Christmas Day. May I set aside all selfishness and turn my attention to those most in need. Amen.

R. Scott Hurd serves as vicar general for the Personal Ordinariate of the Chair of St. Peter. A priest of the Archdiocese of Washington, he is the former executive director of the Archdiocesan Office of the Permanent Diaconate and has also served in the Archdiocesan Office for Religious Education. Hurd began his professional ministry as an Episcopal priest, entered the Catholic Church in 1996, and was ordained a Catholic priest four years later. He and his wife live with their three school-aged children in Alexandria, Virginia. Hurd is the author of *Forgiveness: A Catholic Approach, Daily Devotions for Lent 2013,* and *When Faith Feels Fragile.* Follow Hurd online at fatherscotthurd.blogspot.com.